Paradigm Books

THE INNER TRUTH

Dr. Gurpreet Dhillon has spent many years in academia with positions in UK, Portugal, Hong Kong and the USA. He is a world traveller and enjoys pondering over the joys of life, love and relationships.

The Inner Truth is his first endeavor into the world of poetry. In many ways the book is a dialogue with his inner self, albeit with a poetic narration.

Gurpreet S. Dhillon

THE INNER TRUTH

Paradigm Books

Paradigm Books is an imprint of Aldwych Associates.
2020 Pennsylvania Avenue NW, Ste 904
Washington DC 20006, USA
books@aldwychassociates.com

Made and printed in USA
Typeset in Century Schoolbook
Cover photograph © Gurpreet S. Dhillon

ISBN-13: 978-0615807140 (Paradigm Books)
ISBN-10: 0615807143

For my parents

Contents

Foreword

Family: Friends and Family!
Ravinder S. Kohli

The word family is comforting and emanates security.
We are all fortunate to have a family.
One family is gifted to us with His blessings,
The vesicle are our siblings biological or adopted.
This comes with obligations and mores,
Social, moral and cultural.
Then there is the family we choose to be our family,
With no obligations - just love, respect and a warmth we
cherish,
We wish this family well with no envy - these are our friends.
Then is the family given to us by our children,
A family we give boundless love through our actions - not
words.
All of these give us abundant joy and warm to our souls.
To all these families - inherited and chosen
May God bestow his Grace,
To all we wish them *Sewa*[1], *Sehat*, *Sehaj*,
And above all *Sukh* and *Santokh*.

---

[1] In Punjabi language *Sewa* refers to service, *Sehat* to health, *Sehaj* to
patience, *Sukh* to happiness and *Santokh* to contentment. The five S's are
also part of the teachings of the Sikh Gurus.

Acknowledgements

I was never formally trained in poetry. I was however greatly influenced by William Wordsworth. I loved his rhyming style. The simplicity of Wordsworth's poems was just phenomenal. And yet in his simplicity resided a rather complex romantic thought. While these influences galore, I never had the confidence to share my poems with any one, let alone publish them. Credit for this goes to my wife, Simran. She found a way to convince me and boost my morale, which took me to a point where I agreed to compile them into a book. Thank you my dear. The second person to encourage me to write and compile the poems was our dear friend Mona. She perhaps also felt that there was this urge in me to pen a few lines ever so often. And then Ravi really felt the emotions expressed in many of the poems. My children, Akum and Anjun, have patiently heard me narrate the poems to them. They just believed in me. Thank you all for bearing with my idiosyncrasies, which are hard to explain. Perhaps the collection of poems in this book opens a window to know me better.

Gurpreet Dhillon
April 2013
Richmond, Virginia

A Reflection

I can't remember the first time I wrote poetry. It was perhaps in high school. Somehow the words came naturally. In later years however I attribute it to the strict regime that my high school teacher Brother Hughes, made us follow. The memory of scribbling the meaning and the context within which the poem was written is still fresh in my mind. Brother Hughes would often take us on a journey. One time when we were studying "Ode to a Nightingale" by John Keats, we were virtually transported to the Keats time frame (1796-1821). Keats references to "blushful Hippocrene" was explained as the Greek fountain of the horses and the "winking" in that context was indeed the "twinkling and the sparkling of the sorrows". The analysis was so in depth that never did we realize that we were indeed studying poetry. It was nothing more than beautifully crafted prose.

Then there was this time when I picked up our prescribed poetry book – *Panorama*, published by Oxford University Press in 1974, and scribbled a couplet. Part of the words and sentences were from Robert Browning's "The Pied Piper of Hamelin". It read something like this:

Rossio Square, Lisbon, Portugal

When Cynthia similes, the skies are blue,
The world takes on a roseate hue.
Birds in the garden trill and sing,
And joy is King of everything – when Cynthia smiles.

The cheeks are rosy and the curls flaxen,
Chins with dimples and teeth like pearls.
Tripping and shouting, skipping and laughing,
Makes Cynthia even more beautiful.

For decades this small little poem stayed on the inside back cover of my high school poetry book. And would have stayed there had it not been for my better half to give me a nudge – well this happened rather recently.

Over the years a lot of friends would ask me to scribble a few words for their daughters graduation or the sixteenth birthday. I would do that dutifully. I would transport myself to the child's youth, their mischievousness, and their babyhood clams. These lines would then show up on several birthday cards, acknowledgements and thank you notes. In a few years all our friends knew that I was writing these notes for them. I never signed these poems and some friends tell me that they just knew that it was me.

Do I really have to tell,
When you already know.
Do I have to say,
When you can feel,
Do I really have to justify,
When you already care.

Yet, I never had the confidence to publish my poetic writings. I never felt that they were worth anything. On occasion I would read these poems to my children. I would get some

The Harbor, Barcelona, Spain

encouragement from my 11 year and 7 year olds. But, again I was never sure. Maybe they were just encouraging me and acknowledging the poetry because I was their dad. One fine day, my wife who seemed to be in a rather pensive mood at that moment suggested that why don't I compile my poems into a book. "Really", I said. "Are they worth a dime", I asked. "Yes", she said. And then there was no further acknowledgement. As part of my profession I had written several books, but a poetry book ... this was going to be a first.

Then one day another dear friend of ours visited us. We were generally lounging around after a rather relaxed lunch. My wife happened to mention that I was writing a poetry book. At that moment it just dawned on me that yes indeed I was. As if I was trying to get affirmation, I pulled one of my latest writings on my iPhone via Dropbox and handed the phone over to our friend. She read it, acknowledged it, nodded, smiled, got into a sort of a vacant mood and said, "this is really good. It's deep, with a meaning". I felt good. I showed her another and then another. Finally she said that she would like to suggest a theme for my future writings. "How about Alzheimer's", she said. "I could", I said. Our friend was a little reluctant to suggest this topic area, largely because my mother has Alzheimer's and we are the primary care givers. I had seen my mother transform from being a lady of steel to a fragile, dependent old woman. Every time I think of her, I get sad. Sad at my helplessness. Sad at fate and destiny. And angry at a lot of contextual things. All this usually got combined to depress me, which was however my fodder for the writing.

Modern art ...somewhere is Lisboa!

I was soon to discover that there is a class of poetry, which is *Imagism*. As Ezra Pound once wrote: imagism is "that which presents an intellectual and emotional complex in an instant of time." Ezra Pound was an American expatriate poet, who at one time got so troubled with England's international politicking that he decided to go and live in Italy, albeit to support Mussolini. He was accused of treason by the United States and was also found mentally unfit to stand trial – following his detention for 25 days behind a six-by-six outdoor steel cage. Pound was surely controversial, but his liking for Imagism, which had roots in Chinese and Japanese poetry, is surely a contribution. The path Pound chose may not be well appreciated by a majority of people, but the pain is indeed visible in his works. Similarly there are episodes in ones life, which leave a mark. Painful as these might be, they become a source of inspiration. I call this a consequence of the *Pain Crisis*. Just as individuals discover a different aspect of themselves following a *mid-life* or a *quarter-life* crisis, so does a *pain crisis* result in people thinking differently.

I have had my share of joys and tribulations. Some have been rather easy to deal with, while others somewhat painful. When I step back and look at all things past, I see and feel a sense of Imagism crawling into me. But I am no expert; all I do is interpret what I think it is.

You stand tall,
I just look up,
And admire,
I wish I could reach there,
But, some say I have,
I think otherwise though,

Somewhere on the Holden Beach, North Carolina. I love the convolutions since these signify inherent confusions in an Alzheimer's patient.

For there is so much to learn,
So much to share,
So much to write,
Before I get there.

Much of the inspiration for this book comes from people around me. These are people I care about (or have cared about). These are people who have influenced me – my children, my wife, my parents. I also have a selection of poems, which I wrote at the behest of our friend Mona. These all deal with Alzheimer's and my own journey in dealing with it. These poems are also dedicated to my loving mother who is currently suffering from this terrible disease.

What it is I don't care,
For there is that cure,
I await.
Is it that mutated gene,
Or an inflammation,
That causes this terrible disease.

Times like these, when you care for a loved one, test several relationships – with friends and relatives alike. Those experiences also become an inspiration of sorts. Many a time people stand besides you in this journey, but many a time they don't. It's unfortunately more of the latter. I really thank those who stood besides me or did not. The least they did was to become a source of my inspiration.

Poetry books are very personal. They open a window to your heart and soul. Or, for that matter any person's soul. The question that often arises is – does it matter. It depends who you are talking to. I think it really matters. Poetry is a psychologists' case study to study human nature. It is the *episteme* on which human behavior is founded. It imbibes in

A picture speaks a thousand words. A clash of the turbulent with the reigned.

itself the historical and the emotional. It has a language of its own. It is an expression. What a hundred pages of prose may not be able to convey, a hundred words of poetry do.

I wish I could sing,
Sing a poem.
To convey my meaning,
Than write all those letters.
I wish I could narrate,
A poem.
To show my love to you,
I know the day you got sick,
How could I forget,
But I hope I could sing,
A poem.
To express my love,
To share my feeling,
Of talking to you.
Now I have nothing,
But memories of yester,
And this poem.
I remember when you got hit,
In the head,
And then to forget,
Your past and the present.
I remember all that,
And also that you still remember me.
I cherish the smile I get,
When I walk into your room,
When I hand over a candy,
Or a glass.
All I have is memories,
Of the times when you did the same,
To me.
Now all I have is memories,
And this poem,
To remember you.

Somewhere in the midst of Blue Ridge Mountains, Virginia

I have no clue

I try and forget,
I drown myself in chores,
I wonder what is in store,
When there is no memory,
But, I was recently reminded,
By a dear friend,
That there is disease of sorts,
Not of the heart or the soul,
Not of the physical self,
Not a cancer or an ache,
But that of the mind,
A disease that is stricken,
Malady that's not bedridden,
Yet it's an ailment,
That is hard to describe,
For it's the heart that refuses to confess,
That she is indeed stricken,
One thing is sure though,
She will worsen .... day by day,
And yet I'll be helpless,
For there ain't anything I can do,
To turn the course, if at all,
Even the medicine man took a guess call,
For he had no clue,
As to what caused the sluice,
Of memory and things dear,
But a name it has,
Of something that eats from within,
Alzheimer's or Dementia it might be,
Godforsaken it certainly maybe.

*My mom... as I knew her before
the onset of Alzheimer's*

Thank you mom for being there. And thank you for those wonderful 50 years. I wish you could rejoice with me, as I am doing so now. I know for sure that this is exactly what you would have wanted. I dedicate this book, my past, present and the future to you.

You were my soul,
You were my feeling,
You were my love,
You were my pride.

What has become of you,
What has come on you,
You were a person of steel,
Now at the bottom of the stee.

I want to talk to you,
I want to feel with you,
But alas....

I dedicate this book to you.

*****

Love

The word "love" is an interesting one. First mention of love results in people imagining the physical manifestation of love – commonly referred to as *romantic love*. However recently I was in a conversation with the priest at the local temple. And I happened to ask him, "what is love?" Our conversation resulted in stating something to the following effect: If you do not have any feeling of love for God, you will not love any of His creations. Your heart will be barren. And you will have no compassion. What the priest said was interesting. He, in many ways, intertwined the romantic and the spiritual.

To love is to feel,
To feel is to have compassion,
To be compassionate is to have mercy,
To love the Lord is to touch his feet,
To have his blessings is the love to be.
And that is passion.

Many psychologists however differentiate between *compassion* and *passion*. They consider compassion to include a sense of mutual respect and attachment, affection and trust. Passionate love is characterized by sexual attraction, anxiety and affection.

The Gardens of Versailles, France

Whatever it is,
I am in love,
I am passionate about you.
I can't wait to see you,
I get anxious if you are not there.
Now that you have no memory,
I feel for you,
I have a lot of respect for you,
And I still love you.
You are my mother,
You inspire me,
Even though you are not well,
I do love you.

This part of the book is devoted to all sorts of love poems. Many of these are reflections and offer a mixed dose of compassion and passions. I personally however like love to be viewed as obsessive, realistic and selfless. Many of these themes resonate in my collection.

A prayer

O Lord
The creator of all species and master of all
Lift the hearts of those
For whom he always stood
Take us from painful memory and continued deprivation
To do what he always strived for
O Lord we believe that you will provide for us
In our strive to continue on the path
Our beloved father showed.
And please help us to comfort ourselves
And provide us with fulfillment as:
"Blessed are those who mourn, for they shall be comforted."

Park Güell, Barcelona, Spain

This is a prayer about love for God, the almighty and the savior. It does not matter what religion it belongs to. It is just a prayer asking the beloved good Lord *Waheguru*, to show us the path. I believe I wrote it sometime during my senior years in high school and am certain that it was inspired by what I learned at school. When I was a child growing up in Chandigarh (India), my parents decided that I should be getting a well rounded and a disciplined education. One of the best schools at that time (and perhaps is even today) was St. John's. It was an Irish Catholic Brothers institution, originally founded by Brother Edmund Rice. Each morning we were indoctrinated to recite the Lord's prayer. It can be found in Matthew 6:9-13. A version is also in Luke 11:2-4. Though inspired by the Lords prayer, my version is simply asking *Guru Nanak* to show us the path.

Love is a flower,
We cherish it for ever,
We love the scent,
We worry the sklent.

Love is the joy,
That we usually ploy,
To keep away the fro,
And to pick a crow.

Love is the shiver,
That we rather have never,
For love is the joy,
That need not be a toy.

Unknown. Somewhere in Portugal

What is this love?
When I cant' talk to you.
What is this love?
When I cannot feel with you.
What is this love?
When I can only see you.
What is this love?
When I can just cry for you.

Love is amazing. It means so much. When you don't have it.
You feel for it. When you get it, you take it for granted. This is
what I have come to believe.

I once met a maiden,
Young as she could be,
She was surely sodden,
With grief possibly.

I happened to ask,
What was to torment,
She kept quite and masked,
And appeared like sorbent.

It is the love,
That gets hidden,
With a hove,
Though she was smitten.

Years later,
When nuptials she got,
I met when she was in slatter,
She was surely in a slot.

Love she still had,
That she could not hide,
For me that was bad,
For she wasn't to *bide*.

Inside of La Sagrada Familia by Antoni Gaudi, Barcelona, Spain

Dedication

In all ye years,
I have but yearned,
To share with ye,
The pleasure of thee.

You are the sunshine,
That shivers the spine,
You are the strength,
Taking me to the nth.

You shower the love,
Desirous of thee,
You bring pleasure,
Not worthy of we,

You are my love,
And it will be,
Now and for ever,
It will be.

Bangalore, India

For years I have been a student of semiology – the theory of signs. I was perhaps introduced to the concept in the late 1980s. And ever since have somehow related everything around us to semiotics. My first introduction was a rather complex and difficult to read book by Ronald Stamper, which in later years had been simplified by my advisors Jonathan Liebenau and James Backhouse. However one does need to read Eco Umberto to really understand the nuances. And particularly so behind the backdrop of Nietzsche, whose philosophy was introduced to me by my mentor Ian Angell.

I have never been too good at buying flowers or wearing reds on valentine's. To some extent my wife has always been a little upset with me because of this. However I have always wondered, what is there in a 'sign' or a 'token' which makes people upset? Should they be really upset when they get the expression, the intention and the feeling from an individual. I might extend my assertion to say, what is there in an artifact that makes one more happy than without it?

I guess answers to these questions are way more complex than can be handled in a poetry book. They are worth a thought though. The French sociologist, Bruno Latour, certainly has an opinion when he articulates his *actor network theory*. But, then there might have been a difference between a simple artifact and objects.

Holden Beach, North Carolina

Silent

What is there to care,
It is simply an object,
It is you and me,
Who make sense of it,
Others however debate about it,
Or simply pass it unnoticed,
Whatever the object might be,
It certainly has something to say.

What is this love?
Why this color?
Why this flower?
Why this dinner?
Why this savor?
Why this expression?
Why this candor?
If it is for love...
Color or flower or salver,
Mean not a thing.
If it is love...
It is the unsaid that matters.
If it is love...
Then the feeling is what counts.
If it is love...
It is the deeds that count.

Have a happy Valentine's

Unknown. Somewhere in Spain

She loved her life

When she was struck,
The mind was gone,
I left my home,
To be with her.
Such was the love,
That I wished to sleep with her,
Slumber she did,
But all night called,
Feared for the worst.
In the morning she cried out, O ye vendors
What ye have,
I want the right price for,
What ye have.
I tried to convince,
I tried to console,
I hugged and kissed,
All to hear, O ye maidens
What ye have,
Why ye here,
Leave my son alone,
For he is taken.
Yet again,
I tried to comfort,
I tried to soothe,
All ye to no avail,
For she had no memory,
Of who ye called.

Remnants of Fort Ghungrana in my ancestral village. The fort was controlled by my family. The tower marks the spot where Lord Metcalf had an audience with Maharaja Ranjit Singh in 1804. The Fort was destroyed by the English some 50 years later. My family had sided with the Maharaja in the Battles of Aliwal and Baddowal - a legacy that my father wanted me to preserve.

Many of the narrations in this book relate to my mother. And there has been a limited mention of my Dad. I indeed had a very special relationship with him. He left for his heavenly abode in 1998. Just a couple of months prior to his eternal passage, I visited him from Hong Kong (that is where work had taken me then). In retrospect, he looked tired. On one occasion he mentioned that we should get a family picture done. On another he insisted on getting ready and dressing up prior to a picture session. He had commented then, "these are memories". The following poem is dedicated to my dad - who spoke little, but had substance; who knew all, but never insisted, who maintained a legacy and asked me to carry forward.

I sighed and I sobbed

I sighed and I sobbed
For that I was robbed;
Of a soul that I loved
For whom all the care I showered.

I wailed and I cried
The tears down they hailed;
But nothing is availed
As all our calls failed.

Up and onward shall we move
As he preached while in his hove.
Satisfied he shall feel
When we would achieve
All his aspirations for us.

Unnoticed Beauty at Parque das Nações
Expo Area of Lisboa, Portugal

Unnoticed Beauty

Oh dear....
Thou art so beautiful,
Surrounded by beauty to the full,
Nice and smart are they till,
But thou magnificent remain still.
We like pines gaze at your beauty,
In summer and winter sweetie,
Till you make a treaty,
For all the years as you grow,
Us the moon and stars gaze at your brow,
And admire your beautiful trough.
But oh no! The tragic destiny,
No human eye has seen your serenity,
Unknown you lie,
And unknown you'll fly,
And would pass away unnoticed,
By a human eye.

Barcelona Landscape

Growing up, my mother would always mend my ways and would often exclaim, "don't be obsessive". This was about the time when I began detesting all sorts of obsessive compulsive behaviors. Even as I began loving her even more, especially when she got the disease, I would often hold myself and ask, am I being obsessive? But, is it really negative to be obsessive? I guess not. There is indeed a lot of love in each and every obsession.

Obsession

Obsessed I am I confess,
For I am the stricken,
With a lot of stress,
And I am forbidden,
To call and care,
And be stricken,
Of the love I had,
And the care I gave,
To now feeling and cad,
And yet there is a part of me,
That shall always be love clad.

Could be anywhere

Sadness in love is something we witness everyday. May this be the love of a son or daughter for the parents, a woman for her partner, parent for their child. There are ups and downs in all relations. However what is amazing is to witness the mixed emotions. As I have often pondered about this, I have been reminded of an interesting play, *Endgame*, written by Samuel Beckett. Two of the characters, Nagg and Nell, are portrayed to have an interesting perspective. At one point Nagg talks about an Englishman who is unable to get a tailor to make him a pair of trousers. While the Englishman is more powerful socially, yet he is powerless in getting the tailor to obey him. At another point in the play, his wife Nell says, "Nothing is funnier than unhappiness". While Nagg and Nell are the parents of their "caregiver" son Hamm, yet Hamm himself is disabled. When I read the play, it leaves mixed emotions of love and care, power and control, humor and sadness. And perhaps sadness in love is that manifests itself in many relations.

Sadness in Love

When I saw her smile,
I could tell,
She was happy in style,
But there was this something that fell,
Though her eyes, deep as a Nile,
I could see her unhappy like Nell,
Scared she was to a file,
What is they saw her nail,
With friends and loved ones sail,
To be a women again without fail,
To care, to love, to feel without rale,
And be loved by those who need no Braille,
For she had a lot to offer to those not stale.

Gaudi's Casa Mila, Barcelona, Spain

I fear

I fear thy anger sweet maiden,
You needest not fear mine,
My spirit, thought and mind are too deeply laden,
To ever burden thine.
I always fear thy tours and thy motion,
Still you needest not fear mine,
Immense is my hearts devotion,
With which I worship thine,
True it is from the core of my heart,
From me to thine.

Camp Nou, Barcelona Football Club, Barcelona, Spain

Daughters are amazing. There was this one time when my daughter insisted that I have lunch with her at school. Honestly I wasn't sure. And it was going to be a rather hectic day. I had several meetings and then an evening class to teach. However when I agreed, the twinkle in her eye made my day.

Twinkle

There was this twinkle in her eye,
I have never seen something like that fly,
All she asked was to come have a visit,
To be with her when she feasted,
When I had said I wasn't sure,
I could see that furor,
She kept persisting though,
Till I said I was sure,
I would be there,
To hold hands without fear,
And have lunch,
With my sweet little punch.

How can I not mention my son? One time he broke his glasses. Fuming and spuming he called me. He said, "I need you". "What happened", I said. "I broke my glasses", he said. "I know you can fix them", he continued. "Sure", I exclaimed .... so vehemently that I was perhaps the "superman" with the "super glue". But how can one let the child down.

My dad

Dad is the super man,
Dad is the super glue,
No one is stronger than he,
No one better than him,
He is my dad,
He is my hero,
I love him,
More than a being.

The instance reminded me of my own dad. He had this passion for wrestling. And always wanted me to be strong. On occasion he would promise to buy me something, only if I was strong enough to bend his arm. I have now tried the same trick with my son. It is actually so easy to keep the arm straight... a trick that one learns rather quickly. However until very recently I believed in my dad's strength. I believed in what he told me. Though I lost him to the heavens several years ago, I still believe in him and thank him for everything. As did my own son, recently, when I had fixed his glasses.

The Benfica Eagle

Thank you and Mention not

When I got the call,
He wanted me to be there this fall,
Come running he said,
Forget the leaves he cried,
For I need you now,
I wondered what it would be,
What if something untoward be,
It was just a broken glass,
That he could not just let pass,
I ran to him,
To fix it for him,
And then he showered me,
With all the love you, love me,
Thank you and Thank you,
I left unsure,
Was it love or just to be?

*****

Birth + Day

Over the years I have written several verses signifying birthday's. However it was only recently that I began reading about Eleithyia, the Goddess of Childbirth. In 2012 we had also visited Louvre where a depiction of Eleithyia, Zeus and the birth of Athena exist. Interestingly my trip to Louvre, Paris was proceeded by a visit to Athens and Crete. Legend has it Eleithyia was born in Crete. And there are several references of her in the Homeric poems. It is also believed that when Eleithyia was angry, she prolonged the labor. When she was happy, women had a short labor – as the fable goes. Irrespective of Eleithyia's temperament though there was always a celebration. In ancient history such celebrations have been recorded in the Bible, Ancient Indian scriptures, Babylonian civilizations, amongst others.

As we were preparing for yet another celebration, albeit closer to home, I felt the urge to pen a few lines for my dear friend – Ravi. And on his 60th, I penned a few simple sentences that say it all.

The joy is there,
Tribulations galore,
For you are to fare,
All the splore.

From inside the Louvre, Paris, France

"Splore" we surely did on his birthday. And indeed there was immense frolic and boisterous merrymaking. And how could we ever forget what Ravi and Mala did when our little angel came along. They held her close and we were swept off our feet.

You made our day,
When you held her close,
You made us fay,
For you were to pose,
With that little sway,
To the stows,
You took her,
Before we showed,
And blessed her,
For what we could have crowed.

Connections

I have wondered,
With a bit of surrender,
As to what a relation is?
Is it the affinity?
Is it consanguinity?
Is it by decent?
Is it the rent?
But, then I have also wondered,
And often pondered,
That it is indeed none of those,
That we may pose,
It is indeed the love,
That we define,
Not the blood,
Not the connection,
All those though seem irrelevant,
It is just the feeling that we cherish.

Kerala Back Waters

A child changes your life ... forever. And so it did in 2001. And what ensued says it all.

First One

I am turning ONE!
Oh! It's been fun.
My mom and dad have been getting the brunt.
I wake up when they want to sleep.
I want a change when they are ready to eat.
I spill up when they have just cleaned.
I scream when they want peace.
I want to be picked up when my mom's cooking.
I want to sit in my dad's lap when he is working.
They try to calm me.
They try to pacify me.
They try to explain.
They shout.
They scream.
They pull their hair.
I give them a wicked smile.
With a twinkle in my eye.
They forget the anger.
And give me a hug.
Such is fun.
And I am going to be ONE!

Random coastal shot in Kerala

And then came another one, which added to the joy.

Another one!

I am going to be one,
It's going to be fun.
With fun 'n' frolic,
Music and dance,
Come and help me turn one.

I love cuddling up to my dad,
I like clinging to my mom,
I love playing with my brother's toys,
And always find new ploys,
To be hugged and kissed,
And be missed.

Oh, it's going to be fun,
I am going to be one.

I love helping mom clean up,
And dad to write up,
My dad has taught me to walk,
My mom keeps helping me to talk,
My brother has been a charm.

Oh, it's going to be fun,
I am going to be one.

My daughter's sand castle. A beach in North Carolina

Our Little Darling

Our little darling is going to be three.
Our angel is now on a spree,
From wee hours till we sleep,
She keeps us on our feet.

She is now growing.
From being a baby to a little girl,
Conscious of her looks,
Percipient of her clothes.

But she is our darling.
She is the fascination of her dad,
The princess of her mom,
The joy of her brother.

In Lisboa, Portugal

Our Joy

I am now three
And feel that I am free
The past two years have been tough
I could not tell about a lot of stuff
Was it a shout
Love or scold
Pat or a slap.
Now I am three
I know when I miss my Mom and Dad
When I want a hug
Or when I have done something wrong.

So ...please join me in celebrating my three
We will have fun
We will enjoy
Dance and sing.

Come to my home ...please
For the fun 'n' frolic

Spring - a season that promises happiness and bright futures.
random shot from Virginia

Sashay

It seems like just yesterday,
From a baby wrapped in a blanket,
I have turned two today,
And ready to wear a gantlet.

I am keeping mom and dad on their feet,
I am keeping my brother at bay,
Isn't that sweet,
Especially when I've learned to sashay.

Come let's have fun,
At my home,
On December one,
And get a glimpse of my tome.

An aspect of Gaudi's apartment block

The life indeed got changed with the love of my life. We may not speak about it. We may not talk about it. We may not mention it. The love will remain. The love is there. The care shown in everything you do. But, when it is your birthday, I do have something to share.

Come on!

Come on sweet,
Get ready to throw you a treat,
For it's the nicest day,
To have fun and play.
Nay. It's your birthday,
Thou art may be galore and in sun,
Today's your day to have fun.
So, lets order it in the main,
If we are a bit sane,
Or, have you any other thoughts better,
May be they are even better touts,
Anyhow wish you have a wonderful day.

For several years now conquering the 1776 steps that take you to the top of CN Tower, Toronto, Canada has been a passion of sorts.

Some sort of craziness is imbibed in all of us. Some ten years ago I was introduced to stair climbing by my dear friend Jasvinder. I remember the first time he had invited me to Toronto to 'conquer' the CN Tower. The task seemed daunting, but both of us were well prepared. We had talked about the right proportion of carbohydrates and proteins that would optimize our performance. The following year we even climbed the Sear's Tower in Chicago. Climbing stairs is an addiction. We train throughout the year for a 20 minute gratification. All this is well worth it though. Because of our climbing, Jasvinder and I have formed a special bond (he happens to be a Dhillon too). And when he turned 50, I penciled in a few lines for him.

Over the hill

How many times have you seen a guy go over the hill?
First ...
When he enters the tweens
Second ...
When turns forty
Third ...
When he celebrates five decades of yester years

Yes
My friend is turning half a century old
And we are going to rock the clock.

Please
Join us for the
Giggles and Wiggles
Sparkels and bottoms up!

There is one condition though
No gifts ... gags may be
But, if you must
Get something that we can twinkle with.

Random shot from Kerala, India

And then Jasvinder's daughter turned sixteen. How could it be that I was not going to write something for her.

You are sixteen going on seventeen

We remember when we waited for you,
The impatience and the tribulations,
The palpitations and the pulsations,
Of having you in our arms.
You filled us with all the pleasures,
Our impatience turned into excitement,
Pulsation into joy,
For we could hold you in our arms.

Now you are in your teens,
We worry and get vexed,
We scold and reprimand,
We ask you not to be tetchy,
Of the lads, rogues and the cads,
All because we love you.

We will always look over you,
To prosper and be merry,
To shower intellect and sense.
We will always pray for you,
For each milestone,
For everything you savor,
For each day that opens new doors,
As our little princess blossoms,
You are indeed sixteen going on seventeen.

A view of gardens of Versailles, France that occupy what was once the Domaine royal de Versailles

Some more good wishes were to come when Jasvinder's second daughter tuned sixteen.

Dimpled Chin

We still remember
That dimple
And that smile
She made our day
When she arrived

Sixteen years on
She is our joy
She fills the room
With an aura
That is hard to describe.

She is our baby
The loved one
The youngest one
The carefree one
The mischievous one

We are so happy
That you are turning sixteen
Wish you were still a baby
Who we could cuddle up to
Who you always remain
Our loved one.

Entrance to the Palace of Versailles, France

Sweetness

When you were born
The sweetness was sown

You filled the air
With such a fare

That we had a spray of honeysuckle
Dew on our knuckles

That we could not stop loving you
So that we glance at the dimpled you

Now that we take away our hand
In grass and sand

All we see is your smile
With love in your eyes

Now you are sixteen
And gone is your feen

You will blossom
To be a woman

With all the love
That we will always cherish

Random shots - ancient Spanish architecture

When he had first moved into town, the two Dhillon families discovered each other. We have shared many an interesting times with Manjit and his family. There never has ever been a feeling that we are just friends. They are indeed our family. With Manjit and his family we have shared many fun moments, birthdays and the like. And when Sukhmani turned sixteen, it did indeed deserve a special from me.

Our baby

We look back at the days you were young.
We think of the moments that were unsung.
We cherish the memories galore,
We are awed with your growing lore.
You were our baby, our bitsy wee,
But now you are a lady, no longer a teeny-weenie.

You are now sixteen, going on seventeen,
You are our love. You are our hope,
You are our treasured one,
You will always be our baby.

*One of my favorite heritage sites - Temple Romano de Évora
(also referred to as Templo de Diana, the ancient Roman
Goddess of the moon, the hunt, and chastity)*

Besides the constant encouragement from my wife to write this book, there was only one other person who thought that it was worth the effort. Her encouragement and initial motivation did matter a lot. I may not have expressed that to her, but Mona was one of the reasons that made me feel that I could indeed get this project off the ground. As a family we have always shared special moments with Mona and Raj's kids. The younger one, Veer, is indeed a mischievous brat. On one occasion he came running to me. I was contemplating a hug. Little did I realize that he was actually going to bite me. What had I done Veer? Nevertheless the instance had to be hardcoded into his fifth birthday poem.

The fifth

It was yesterday,
When we had a blessed day,
For he was to come and say,
Words that would make you sway.

Now five years on,
He has certainly shone,
To be that one,
Who we cherish as a pone.

The cutie pie is the one we want to eat,
But that hug of his with stretched feet,
Makes you sit on your seat,
And the hug to crying hughie comes neat.

We love your smile though,
For you bring sunshine through stow,
And bring that ray to know,
That you are there to forge as prow.

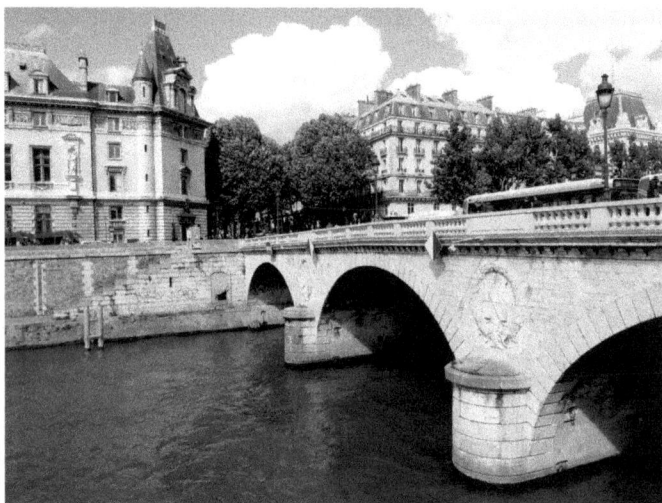

Bridge over River Seine, Paris

Our love for you is immense,
Though you give in little stence,
You were our little once,
And will be the baby from whence.

The frolic that awaits,
Is certainly going to excite,
So please join us,
For that wonderful sight.

Meaningful

This was the place,
This was the séance,
Where you came,
For her to remain sane,
For my being,
And your seeing,
For that shower and ray of hope,
That all had to cope,
For little did they know,
That I was to be in a flow,
For you to bundle and tope.
Someone did say,
Some bit later,
That I would run and stun,
And give more fun,
Now that I'll be five,
I am looking at that stive,
That you will provide,
To make the day,
For my mom and dad.
And I promise ye all,
A lot of fun and some more stunen.

*****

Lost

It took me a while to classify a bunch of poems that I had written on different occasions. My wife calls some of these "depressing at best". I feel that they reflect reality. I have often told her that being happy all the time may actually be unnatural. While I would make such an assertion largely in support of my so called "depressing" poems, there was indeed some merit in my argument. This got validated when a psychiatrist friend pointed me to a 2011 article published in the *Journal of Positive Psychology*, which related mental disorders with happiness.

My intention in looking up the article in the *Journal of Positive Psychology* was not to continue writing depressive poems, but to really focus on the not so positive side of our lives – things that we usually do not like talking about. In particular I am identifying issues such as broken relationships, failed marriages, getting a suspension in school and the the like. These are very real issues, but we often do not talk about them. People generally feel that by not talking about them brings comfort. I however believe that talking or writing about such issues helps a person vent his or her feelings, which may be therapeutic.

The collection of poems in this chapter have a small real life story linked to them. At times I will provide a narrative, but at others I would just leave it to the imagination of the reader.

Kerala coastline

You are free to draw interpretations, which may or may not have been what I intended.

The following poem relates to the discovery of my mom's cancer.

Something wasn't right

You were fine when I left you,
You were merry when I said bye to you,
You were full of life when I bid adieu,
But when I called you from the South,
You seemed to have a tremor,
Your voice was not yours.
You fumbled at best,
I asked you what was the cause,
"Nothing", you had said
And I knew then,
Something was not right,
Only to discover,
The rot inside,
You had to be rushed,
Across the seven seas,
For an opinion and the scalpel,
And you continue to live,
With the scars and the like,
Even till today,
I knew it then,
That something wasn't right,
I know it now,
That nothing will be right.

Very near the black limestone formations near Hell in Grand Cayman

Realization

It is nice to see some ol' folks,
For they cherish the memories galore,
It is always nice to talk and feel,
Though what they say makes you kneel.

Yesterday was one such day,
When limerick was defined to stay,
For me though it had little relevance,
I just scribble the sentence.

She said it was an anapaest at best,
I thought of the violated prosody in rest,
She said there was some assonance test,
To me it was constant refrain a pest.

What ever it might be,
For me it is the joy to see,
That there is an expression to share,
With those that I care.

Eiffel Tower - an alternative view

There was a time

There was this moment when
she wanted me,
There was this time when she
had to be with me,
There was this care, always for me
There was this feeling that
her world was me.

I still remember the day there
was this bicker,
She was in this spar that nothing
but a brabble,
For her it was a fight to fest,
For she wanted to go to her nest.

Little did I knew then,
That her mind was beginning to fen,
How could I not see,
That her mind was going steel.

Indeed I was trying to be in the present,
But she had already moved
on from the current,
To where her mind took – *tener suerte*.
Yet I kept trying to keep her present.

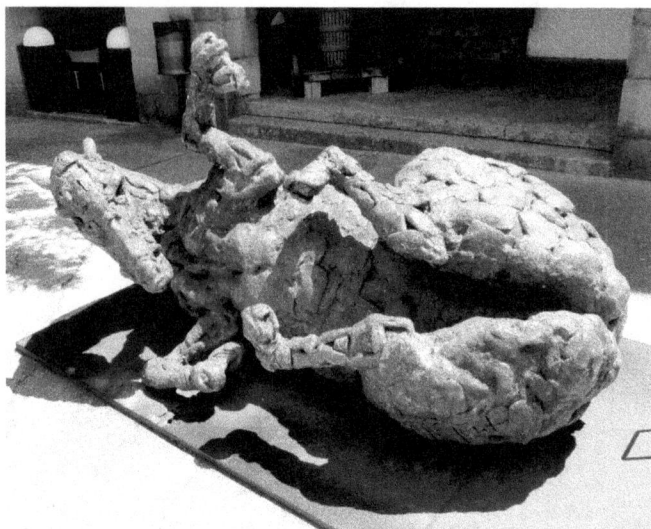

Estadi Olímpic de Montjuïc, Barcelona, Spain

The wilting flower

There was once a flower, a strong
and sturdy one,
Was it a Shasta Daisy or a Petunia?
A Hydrangea, Yarrow or the
Heavenly Bamboo.
One thing was sure it could withstand a lot.

Then one day the wind blew,
No it was a storm for sure,
It ripped though the leaves,
It brought havoc to the steel.

Flowers that were once elegant and smart,
Plants that had compassion a lot,
Stems that were sturdy to the blow,
Gave way for this sea of rain, which poured.

Plants recover, flowers bloom,
Even when it is a pouring gloom,
But when it is your own kind, your own sap,
The wilt continues, till the flower is dead.

Such is the story of one flower,
That was so full of life,
Who always thought of the love she had,
But lost all of it in one blow.

The seed of love is still there though,
It always shall remain there,
Awaiting for that moisture of love,
To germinate and flow once more.

May God have mercy on the sturdy flowers,
For even when the strongest winds drape,
The leathery exterior preserves the inside,
It is a flower of love after all.

The magic square on the façade of Sagrada Familia. The magic constant is 33, signifying the age of Jesus at the time of Passage

There was this ego

I was once told a story,
Simple was the message,
Yet difficult it was to comprehend.

The story had such a deep meaning,
But, no one tried to understand,
For there was a block.

There was once a donkey,
In need of care,
He was offered salt for the cure.

For lack of knowing what was good,
The donkey hit the giver,
Thinking that they were hurting him.

Such is the story of those,
Who think better,
Who deem superior.

It is the ego,
That comes in the way,
To understand what is better.

Alas, sorry I feel,
For the donkey,
Who did not understand.

An unconventional shot of Sangradia Familia, Barcelona, Spain

Anger

I got a little angry today,
Largely because of a stiddy,
There was this person,
Who seemed to be in serzone,
I feel though,
She could not doth,
Anything without being the goth,
Else she would consider,
Without a didder,
That she has to stand besides a tidder,
Someone who is scared,
Of the one who married a lass stared,
And has abandoned, without being faired,
What kind of a person is he,
Who can stand and stare at me,
Someone who has a backbone to be.

When I found myself

They were expressions of my self,
Which became an elf.

For me these were feelings,
Some considered them to be heeling.

I wondered if they were worth anything,
Others considered them to be something.

I wanted them to be really true,
For they expressed my inner rue.

A loved one got worried though,
That I was depressed forth.

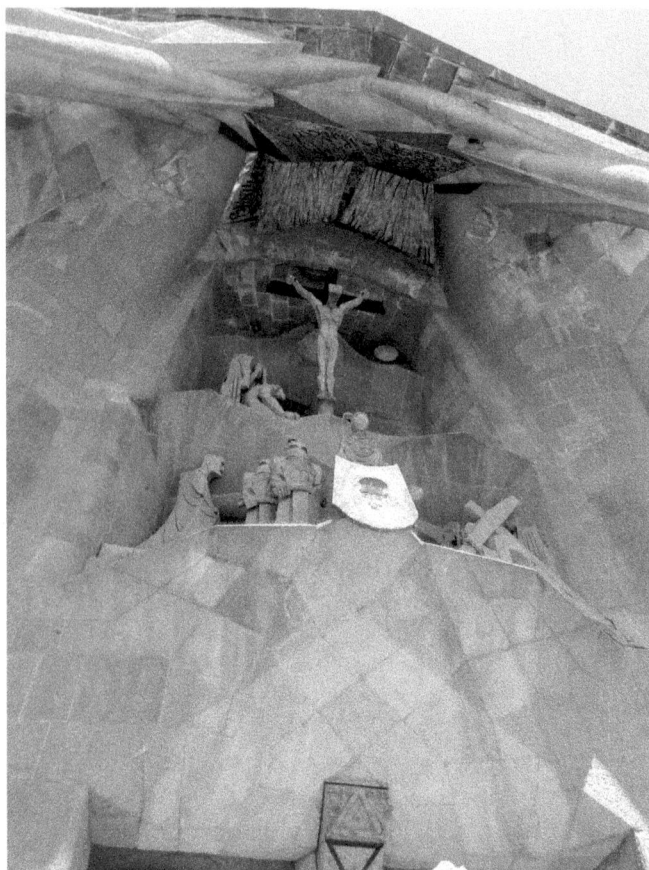

Inside of Sangradia Familia, Barcelona

I may have been,
The poetry though was seen.

I was told that it was worth a try,
To get the word out of the fry.

I agreed reluctantly,
And picked a few selectedly.

The response I got was rather sweet,
There were people who considered it to be treat.

I felt nice,
That there was a price.

Which many appreciated,
For what I have penned reluctantly.

I am now eager and bright,
To get the word out right.

That there is this being,
Who is worth seeing.

For what he has to say,
The heart, love and care to stay.

And be remembered for,
The pain and the stour.

Inside of Sangradia Familia, Barcelona

Can I ever be calm?

There is a calm before the storm,
The leaves remain unruffled in form.
They said we should remain calm,
In spite of the impending storm!
How can I be serene,
When I can see the evolving scene.
He was such a pillar,
With whom I had spend many a stiller.
Yet everyone wants me to remain clam,
When I know there is an impending storm.
Oh Lord, show me the path,
For I want to weather the squall.
Oh Lord, maketh me the path,
For I can't remain anymore in this swathe.

Lady Liberty, New York

Freedom

Don't let that tear come,
Don't let that heart come,
For you are certainly one,
You have something special to come.
As I always say,
Be strong and stay,
For there is yet a day,
That will come to pay.
To get you there,
You can stare,
At the bygones in fair,
And that you were out of the snare.

The storm

There is this unusual clam,
The wind is gone,
And I can hear the tranquil storm,
Yet the sun has not shone.
It is an amazing feeling,
A feeling of mixed passions,
Joy, happiness and serenity I am feeling,
Turmoil, chaos and madness of emotions.
There is this unusual clam,
The wind is gone,
But the storm will disrupt the calm,
It will not be the same for the feeling is gone.
I wish mankind could overcome the storm,
Through love and compassion,
Being honest and being truthful,
For that is the only way we can overcome the storm.

Abandoned boat. Somewhere in Kerala, India

I remember that day so distinctly. It was a Saturday. The Fall leaves had just been cleared. The morning air was crisp and fresh. There was an occasional bird that was chirping. And I was looking out of the window while sipping my tea. I reflected on the years gone by, the love I had, the feelings I cherished. I simply had to write. Or, rather compose.

When I had finished, I wanted to share my feelings with my friends. Twenty years ago I would have simply gone over to a friends house. In today's interconnected world however the meaning of 'sharing' has become synonymous to *facebooking* – where one shares pictures and stories with a rather elaborate group of friends via social media. So, just as the younger generation do, I *facebooked*. And posted my poem. Within minutes I had a bunch of my friends call me. Many expressed concern for my well being. I was truly touched. These were indeed all the people who genuinely cared about me. At that point I just but had to write a follow-up poem to reassure my concerned friends that I was perfectly fine.

The following two poems are part of this discourse.

Missing you

I think of you every day,
When I eat and drink and stay,
At home or office, work or pleasure,
You are in my thoughts even in leisure,
I remember the good times we had together,
I cherish the memories of yester,
Then you went your way,

Fishermen. Keral Backwaters, India

Mine took a foray,
I discovered a new life,
You got drenched in your strife.
In years that went by,
I however remembered you standing by,
Voice full of passion,
Love full of devotion,
Then something happened,
You got hammered,
By the ugly little something,
Not sure what to call it though,
For I am lost for words and thought,
I am unsure of what you mean,
For me it's all about seeing,
The love you had and joy we shared,
Now on this Thanksgiving,
Like many before,
I remember you, your loving charm,
I miss you being around,
Even when I frowned,
I miss your loving touch,
Even when I was stouched,
To my own thing,
You were always there,
To pull me apart,
And let me make sense from the start.
All I know is that I miss you immensely,
Today and will do so forever.

Kerala Back Waters, India

Your care

The poem that I wrote,
Got all my friends to stroke,
I was simply in a stoom,
Thinking of that stone,
That I once cared for,
Cherished from my core,
But I scared another loved one,
For she feared my feeling to cun,
I was simply expressing,
Feeling and deliberating,
About the one I cared,
About the one with whom I shared,
I even got a message,
Concern it was about my pesage,
Another challenged me,
Of the macho me,
What can I say,
But, thank you yay.
For all the concerns you have shown,
For all the love you've given.
I am just a being of yonder,
Waiting for the fonder,
I appreciate though,
The care and thought,
That you carry,
I am indeed pretty and stere-

Via the Vasco da Gama bridge in Lisbon, Portugal

I know it is hard

There was this friend,
Who was in dire need,
Her life began falling,
Right in front of all,

She had no money,
She had no clothes,
All her savings were gone,
Just because of a wretched ol' man.

Her pillar of support got shattered,
Because of the storm,
She had no where to go,
So she called.

What should she do,
Where should she go,
Where was that support,
Who would listen.

There were indeed more questions,
There were more doubts,
There was more concerns,
There was this somber.

Then finally she called,
And said, "I need you",
I want you to listen,
I want to lean.

I want to cry,
I want to be comforted,
I want to be loved,
And I want to be cared.

Megalithic Stones in Alentejo

Help me please,
Help me to overcome,
Help me to sail through,
For I am in troubled waters.

All the big ships have simply sailed by,
All the small ones have been rocked,
By this ol' man and woman,
Who simply shattered my dreams.

It was hard for her to ask for help,
It was hard for her to confess,
That suddenly from being rich at heart,
Poor she was in everything.

We told her to be calm,
For in our hearts we knew,
That the Lord maketh a path,
For those who love Him,

But did these lines of comfort mean a thing,
She needed us now,
For money and kind, love and care,
Or... just a hug to say, "we care".

That did not come,
And she was on her own,
We tried to remind her,
That this was just the beginning.

Why not embrace the harsh world,
And stop the cursing,
Why not love the forlorn,
And seek the pleasures of the tranquil.

For there is this long road,
Where you will be alone,
Love your life to the full,
And make new bonds with those who care.

Somewhere in Key West, Florida

I intentionally kept this as the last poem of this book. While the message is rather personal, I suppose it applies to all of us. May it be with respect to relationships, people or places, memories are indeed abound.

Memories

What a day,
When it seems like a fay,
I look around and say nay,
In dismay.
This was the place,
Where we danced,
Where we sang,
And promised a stance.
The memories are glore,
The picture is in store,
Of the happy times,
That were to chime.
But then something happened,
All were saddened,
At what was to transpire,
For that would change,
The course of life forever.

*****

Postscript

The year was 1998 and I was lounging around in La Salle Court in Hong Kong. Earlier in the day I had hopped into the cab and had instructed the driver – *Sing Se Dai Ho* – meaning an institute of higher learning. I was on my way to the City University of Hong Kong. Classes had just begun and I was all prepped up for the upcoming semester. Little did I know that I was going to wrap things up almost immediately and leave for India. My father had suffered a massive heart attack.

The following day when when I was at the Chek Lap Kok airport, I was not in my usual happy mood. There was this numbness that was all over me. I was not sure as to what my father's death meant. Loss of a parent is difficult. To see their suffering is even worst. Ever since my graduation from the London School of Economics, my father had always insisted that I move across the pond to the US. I was however unsure. Somehow the Pacific Rim seemed more exciting. This was soon to change though. I was gradually giving in to my father's wishes.

The second time when I had that uneasiness was when I learnt that my mother had a stroke. This was in 2006. She had been transported to London. I just could not come to terms with myself and had this desire to be with her. I had flown to London over the weekend to see her. And then to eventually get her home.

Vasco da Gama Bridge over River Tagus, the longest bridge in Europe.

Couple of years ago my mother-in-law was diagnosed of cancer and had to undergo intensive chemotherapy. While she is not absolutely cancer free today, one can however see progress. Then just a few weeks ago we came to know that my father-in-law had Metastatic Adenocarcinoma. I could see that same chill run through my wife. I then insisted that she go and spend time with her dad.

These are all major life events. And I compose these words in utter grief, thinking of my parents, my wife's parents, their legacies and what our children will go through.

This one for my dad, who once took me to a stationers shop and I got my first fountain pen ....

> You were the one,
> When you bought me once.
> How can I forget,
> The utter fret,
> That came upon me,
> When you said 'maybe',
> How can I forget,
> That fountain in the pen,
> That I cherished more than a sten.

This one is for my wife ....

> She cherishes those memories,
> Of the food and the bliss,
> Of the *halva*,
> And the like.
> She cherishes that love,
> The care and the hugs,
> That you have always,
> Showered on her.

Évora, Portugal city center from 57 BC when the Romans had conquered the town

She cherishes the quietness,
That surrounds you,
When you are not too pleased.
She cherishes that 'switching off',
When you are not interested.
She cherishes the love,
For soccer and the life,
That you have instilled in her.

And this is for the children in the family ....

Proud you made us,
When we saw the connection,
From Hazura to Gandhi,
From Benoni to back,
Proud we are of the heritage you gave,
From Baldev to Tehal to Bir to Mehtab,
Proudly we will preserve the memories,
Of all things galore.

Over the past few years I have been thinking hard of the relationships – some that you are born with and others that you form.

You argue and then you love,
You fight and you hug,
You hate the fighting in the love,
You like the fighting in the love.
Such is I guess the power of love,
Love that got passed down,
Love from the mom and dad alike,
Love among the siblings,
Why is it then that things fall apart?
Why is it then that love gets lost?
Why is it we stop talking?
And begin thinking ...
Of the Me,
The My,
The Myself.

*****

www.ingramcontent.com/pod-product-compliance
Lightning Source LLC
Chambersburg PA
CBHW060942040426
42445CB00011B/969